SEX EDUCATION FOR 8-12 YEAR OLDS

AN ESSENTIAL GUIDE FOR PARENTS TO RAISING SEXUALLY INFORMED KIDS

BY

JOANNA C. THOMAS

Joanna C. Thomas

Copyright © Joanna C. Thomas 2023

All rights reserved. No part of this book may be reproduced or transmitted in any form or by any means, electronic or mechanical, including photocopying, recording, or by any information storage and retrieval system, without permission in writing from the publisher.

This book is for educational purposes only and is not intended as a substitute for medical or psychological advice, diagnosis, or treatment. Always consult with a healthcare professional before starting any new diet or exercise program.

The information provided in this book is believed to be accurate and reliable at the time of publication. However, the author and publisher do not assume any responsibility for errors, omissions, or for any consequences resulting from the use of the information contained in this book.

Every effort has been made to ensure that all images used in this book are licensed for commercial use. If any images have been used inadvertently without proper licensing, please contact the publisher to rectify the situation.

TABLE OF CONTENTS

INTRODUCTION — 4

CHAPTER ONE — 6

Some One Else Will do it If You Don't — 6
Introduction to the importance of sex education — 10
Dangers and Risks of Not Having the Talk — 12
Addressing common fears or hesitations parents may have about discussing sex education with their children — 14

CHAPTER TWO — 18

You Are the First Role Model — 18
Examining the impact parents have on their children's attitudes towards sex — 19
Ways to model healthy sexual behaviors and attitudes for your child — 21
Common mistakes parents make when discussing sex education with their children — 23

CHAPTER THREE — 26

Understanding Your Child - Setting the Stage — 26
Changes that occur during puberty and how they impact your child's understanding of sex — 27
The importance of building a strong relationship with your child before having "the talk"" — 30
Addressing common misconceptions about sex that tweens may have — 34

CHAPTER FOUR — 38

BEGINNING THE CONVERSATION ABOUT SEX, BODY AND RELATIONSHIPS — 38
DISCUSSING THE BEST WAYS TO START THE CONVERSATION WITH YOUR CHILD — 42
ADDRESSING COMMON QUESTIONS YOUR CHILD MAY HAVE ABOUT SEX AND RELATIONSHIPS — 43
PROVIDING AGE-APPROPRIATE INFORMATION AND RESOURCES FOR YOUR CHILD TO LEARN MORE — 47

CHAPTER FIVE — 50

HOW MUCH TALK CAN BE TOO MUCH — 50
BEST WAYS TO ANSWER YOUR CHILD'S QUESTIONS WITHOUT OVERWHELMING YOUR KIDS — 54
HOW TO PROVIDE ACCURATE INFORMATION WITHOUT BEING TOO EXPLICIT — 55
ADDRESSING COMMON CONCERNS PARENTS HAVE ABOUT DISCUSSING SENSITIVE TOPICS WITH THEIR CHILDREN — 57

CHAPTER SIX — 60

THE INFLUENCE OF THE MEDIA AND WHAT YOU CAN DO ABOUT IT — 60
THE IMPACT OF MEDIA ON TWEENS' UNDERSTANDING OF SEX AND RELATIONSHIPS — 62
ADDRESSING COMMON STEREOTYPES AND MISCONCEPTIONS PERPETUATED BY THE MEDIA — 65
PROVIDING STRATEGIES FOR HELPING YOUR CHILD NAVIGATE MEDIA MESSAGES ABOUT SEX AND RELATIONSHIPS — 67

CHAPTER SEVEN — 70

SEXUAL SAFETY AND SELF-PROTECTION — 70
DISCUSSING THE IMPORTANCE OF CONSENT AND HEALTHY BOUNDARIES — 71
DISCUSSING THE IMPORTANCE OF CONSENT AND HEALTHY BOUNDARIES — 74
COMMON CONCERNS PARENTS HAVE ABOUT THEIR CHILD'S SAFETY — 75

CHAPTER EIGHT — 78

GENDER ISSUES AND IDENTITY — 78
THE IMPORTANCE OF UNDERSTANDING GENDER AND SEXUAL IDENTITY — 79
PROVIDING RESOURCES FOR HELPING YOUR CHILD EXPLORE THEIR IDENTITY — 81
ADDRESSING COMMON CONCERNS PARENTS HAVE ABOUT GENDER AND SEXUAL IDENTITY — 82

CHAPTER NINE — 84

QUESTIONS LIKELY TO BE ASKED AND HOW TO ANSWER THEM — 84
PREPARING YOURSELF — 84

CONCLUSION — 92

FINAL THOUGHTS — 92

INTRODUCTION

As a parent, you want your child to grow up to be happy, healthy, and well-informed individuals.

Part of that means having important conversations about sex and relationships. It's natural to feel a little unsure about how to approach these topics, especially when it comes to talking to your tweens.

That's why we wrote this book - to provide a comprehensive guide to sex education that helps parents navigate these sometimes difficult conversations. Our book covers everything from puberty and sexual health to relationships and consent.

We've included case studies and practical advice to make the material both informative and engaging for tweens.

So if you're looking for a way to start the conversation and ensure your child is well-informed about these important topics, we encourage you to buy this book.

This book will help you with...

Improved communication: By reading this book, parents can learn how to communicate more effectively with their tweens about sex and relationships. This can lead to increased trust, stronger relationships, and better decision-making.

Greater knowledge: Many parents may feel unsure about how to discuss sex and relationships with their tweens, particularly if they were not taught about these topics themselves. This book can provide parents with the knowledge and resources they need to answer their child's questions and provide accurate information.

Confidence: Parenting can be challenging, particularly when it comes to sensitive topics like sex and relationships. By reading this book, parents can gain the confidence they need to approach these conversations with their tweens in a positive, constructive way.

Support: Sex education can be a daunting task for parents to tackle alone. This book provides additional resources and guidance for parents and tweens alike, ensuring that they have the support they need to navigate these topics successfully.

Overall, this book aims to empower parents to have meaningful conversations with their tweens about sex and relationships, providing the knowledge, resources, and confidence they need to support their child's growth and development in this area.

CHAPTER ONE

Some One Else Will do it If You Don't

Although discussing sexual education can be awkward for both parents and children, it's a necessary part of growing up.

Open and honest discussions about sex and relationships are especially crucial when it comes to tweens. According to a proverb, "If you don't do it, someone else will."

So let's investigate this subject and discover why sex education for tweens is crucial as well as how parents may have "the talk" with their children without feeling uncomfortable.

The stakes are really high when it comes to sex education. According to studies, children who receive a thorough sex education are more likely to put off having sex, utilize contraception when they do have sex, and have better relationships.

On the other hand, children who don't receive sex education are more likely to experience sexual assault, STDs, and unwanted pregnancy.

Many parents are still unwilling to talk to their children about sex in spite of these dangers.

Talking about sex may make them feel awkward or embarrassed, or parents may be concerned that it may encourage their children to engage in sexual activity.

But in reality, young people are fascinated about sex and will go for knowledge from a variety of sources, including friends, the media, and the internet.

Consider the situation of 12-year-old Alex, whose parents never taught him anything about sex. He started looking into pornography after seeing some online one day.

Although he had no idea what he was seeing, he was captivated. Before he realized it, he was spending hours online and reading material that wasn't just unsuitable for his age, but was also false and unrealistic.

Unfortunately, Alex's experience is not unusual. Kids have greater access to information than ever in the digital era, but not all of it is reliable or appropriate.

Without adequate sex education, children may seek out harmful material, which can have detrimental effects.

What is the best way for parents to have "the talk" with their tween without appearing awkward or embarrassed? Here are a few advices:

Begin early. Talking to your child about their body and how it functions is never too early. When discussing bodily parts, use the correct anatomical terminology, and be honest and age-appropriate in your responses to your child's queries.

Maintain a mature audience. The degree of detail in your conversations should increase as your youngster matures. When teaching your child about puberty and reproduction, start out simply and progressively add more knowledge as they become older.

Use ordinary occurrences as teaching opportunities. For instance, if your child and you are watching a movie or TV show together and there is a sex scene, using this as an opportunity to discuss consent and healthy relationships.

Be truthful. If your youngster asks a question that you're not sure how to answer, it's acceptable to say "I don't know." The information can always be looked up later combined.

Utilize publications and other tools. You can talk to your youngster about sex and relationships using the many excellent books and online tools available to you. These resources can also offer precise information that you might not feel confident sharing on your own.

Continue having this conversation. Sex education is a continuous discussion that should go throughout your child's adolescence and beyond. It is not a one-time talk.

Additionally, it's critical to keep in mind that sex education encompasses topics such as healthy relationships, consent, and self-esteem in addition to sex mechanics.

By discussing these issues with your child, you may aid in the development of a positive sexual identity and the acquisition of the knowledge and skills necessary for sound decision-making.

It's crucial to monitor your child's media use in addition to having chats with them. It's vital to be aware of the messages kids are hearing since the media can have a big impact on how they view sex and relationships.

Talk to your kids about the pictures and messages they encounter on social media, in movies, and in TV shows, and encourage them to acquire the critical thinking skills necessary to analyze and question these messages.

Talking to your youngster about sexual safety and self-defense is also crucial.

Teach children about consent and limits, and assist them in gaining the self-assurance and assertiveness they need to stand their ground when they sense danger or discomfort.

In discussions about sex and relationships, it's critical to be conscious of gender issues and concerns of identity.

Support your child as they negotiate the complicated world of gender and sexuality and encourage them to explore their own identity.

Sex education for tweens is an important aspect of growing up, but it can make parents uncomfortable to talk about. If parents don't have "the talk" with their children, someone else probably will—and that person might not have the right knowledge.

Parents may help their child develop a positive attitude toward sexuality, the skills they need to make healthy decisions, and the self-defense mechanisms they require by having open and honest interactions with them.

Despite being an uncomfortable subject, it has potential for long-term advantages.

Introduction to the importance of sex education

Are you prepared to delve into the world of tween sex education? Sex education is an essential component of a tween's growth, as uncomfortable as it may be for some parents.

To offer your kids the skills and knowledge they need to make wise decisions in the future, it's crucial to start talking to them about sex and relationships at an early age.

Let's begin with the fundamentals. Learning about human sexuality, including anatomy, reproduction, sexual health, and relationships, is the main focus of sex education.

Understanding our body, our emotions, and our connections with others are all important components of sex, in addition to the physical act itself.

So why is sex education for tweens so crucial?

Let's face it, the world has changed significantly since we were young.

Tweens are exposed to a lot of information about sex and relationships thanks to their access to the internet, social media, and other types of media, some of which may not be factual or suitable.

You can assist your children in navigating this complex world and making educated decisions about their sexual health by supplying them with correct and age-appropriate information.

Now, you might be wondering – when should I start talking to my child about sex? The answer is simple: start early! It's recommended that parents start talking to their children about sex when they are between the ages of 8 and 10.

At this age, children are curious and open to learning, and they are starting to experience physical changes in their bodies.

But what topics should you cover in sex education? Well, that depends on your child's age and maturity level. For tweens, topics may include anatomy, puberty, reproduction, contraception, consent, and healthy relationships. By covering a range of topics, you can ensure that your child has a well-rounded understanding of human sexuality.

Speaking of consent – why is it so important to talk about this with your tween? Teaching tweens about consent is crucial because it helps them understand that they have the right to say no to unwanted sexual advances.

It also helps them learn to respect the boundaries of others and develop healthy communication and negotiation skills. By teaching your tween about consent, you can help them build healthy relationships based on respect and understanding.

What are the repercussions of not having a conversation with your preteen about sex education? Unfortunately, there may be serious repercussions.

Children may seek knowledge from peers or the media if parents don't talk to them about sex education. This may result in false information and unsafe actions including unprotected sex, early sexual activity, and sexually transmitted diseases.

In conclusion, parents must give their children accurate and age-appropriate knowledge on sex and relationships because it is a vital component of a tween's growth.

You may assist your tween in developing a positive attitude toward sexuality and in making decisions about their sexual health by starting the talk early and covering a variety of topics. It's never too early to start the conversation, so don't be scared to do so!

Dangers and Risks of Not Having the Talk

It can be uncomfortable to bring up the subject with your child, I know. But I assure you, it's crucial. Furthermore, the dangers of avoiding "the talk" are not to be taken lightly.

Let's examine some of the risks in more detail, shall we? Your youngster may be more inclined to participate in unsafe sexual practices if they are not given the necessary sex education.

And while unprotected sex is undoubtedly an issue, it's not the only one. The risk of STIs and unwanted pregnancy can be increased by early sexual activity, multiple sexual partners, and using drugs or alcohol before to intercourse.

However, the dangers transcend beyond one's physical health. Your child may be more prone to emotional and psychological suffering if they don't understand consent, boundaries, and healthy connections.

Even that does not account for the effects of inflated expectations and unfavorable social stigma.

I understand what you're probably thinking, though: "But my child is too young for this conversation." Or "They'll learn about it in school." But the reality is that sex education need to begin at home. And it ought to begin right away.

According to research, kids who get thorough sex education from their parents are more likely to put off having sex and to use protection when they do.

Additionally, by being upfront and honest with your child, you may assist them in navigating the frequently complex world of relationships and sexuality. You can give them factual information, remove common misunderstandings, and equip them with the knowledge they need to make wise choices regarding their own bodies and romantic relationships.

Do you need additional evidence? How about the following example? a youngster who had an unprotected pregnancy at age 16 since she wasn't completely aware of the dangers.

She felt ashamed and alone when faced with an unanticipated pregnancy because neither her parents nor her school had ever given her a thorough sex education.

So let's speak about sex and not simply what happens between bees and birds. Let's talk about good communication, consent, and relationships.

Let's discuss the value of protection and the dangers of sex without it. Let's give our kids the tools they need to make wise decisions and lead fulfilling lives.

Addressing common fears or hesitations parents may have about discussing sex education with their children
Let's face it, discussing sex education with your child is not the most exciting subject.

However, it need not be tedious or uncomfortable! In reality, you can help your child comprehend and remember the crucial information they need to know by approaching the subject in a fun and engaging way.

Here are some suggestions for dispelling frequent concerns or reluctances parents may have about engagingly discussing sex education with their kids:

Using narrative: Use of anecdotes or stories to highlight the value of sex education is one technique to make the discussion more interesting.

You may, for instance, tell the tale of a friend or relative who, due to a lack of knowledge about safe sex practices, unintentionally became pregnant or contracted a STI.

Make it participatory: Making the dialogue interactive is another approach to make it more interesting.

Explain the various bodily components or the operation of contraception with the aid of props, sketches, or diagrams. To help your youngster practice saying "no" or making wise decisions, you might also employ role-playing or situations.

Include humor: Discussing sex need not be a serious topic. To help lighten the atmosphere and make the discourse more approachable, utilize comedy. Just make sure the comedy is age- and maturity-appropriate for your youngster.

Focus on values: Tying the discussion back to your family's values is another effective method to make it more interesting.

You could mention that respecting yourself and others entails making thoughtful choices regarding your body and interpersonal interactions, for instance.

You might also discuss how being responsible and caring for both yourself and your partner means engaging in safe sex.

Case Study: A mother chose to teach her kid about sex education by using a board game. She designed a game board with many spots denoting various subjects, including anatomy, birth control, and healthy relationships.

Her son could roll the dice, travel around the board, and respond to questions to gain points. Her son was able to learn and remember the knowledge more readily by making the interaction more engaging and enjoyable.

Sex education doesn't have to be uninteresting or uncomfortable, despite the fact that it may not be the most fascinating topic.

You may make the talk more interesting and memorable for your child by employing narrative, making it interactive, adding comedy, and emphasizing values. Therefore, don't be reluctant to use your imagination and have fun while educating your youngster about sex education!

CHAPTER TWO

You Are the First Role Model

You are your child's first and most significant role model as a parent. When it comes to sex education, this is particularly true because children learn from what they see and hear.

You may lay a solid foundation for your child's understanding of sex and relationships by setting an example of healthy interactions and transparent communication.

Parents can set a good example for their children by modeling positive interactions and honest communication.

Manifest affection being affectionate with your partner in front of your child is one method to set an example for them of healthy relationships.

Simple acts like holding hands, hugging, or kissing can accomplish this. You can model healthy physical affection for your child by displaying it yourself in a caring and respectful manner.

Talk honestly and openly with your partner about sex and relationships as another method to set an example for good partnerships.

You may demonstrate to your child that sex is a common and natural aspect of life by talking to them about these subjects in a courteous and nonjudgmental way.

Your youngster can ask questions and seek advice in this environment that is both open and safe.

Set boundaries: Demonstrating healthy relationships also requires respecting your partner's boundaries and establishing your own.

You can aid your child in developing sound communication skills that will benefit them in all facets of their life by teaching them how to respectfully express their wants and boundaries.

Case Analysis: A parent routinely spoke with his daughter the value of having boundaries and honoring those of others.

His daughter was able to express her boundaries clearly and forcefully when she was in a relationship and felt uneasy about her partner's actions. She was able to keep up a positive relationship and prevent any harm as a result.

Parents serve as their children's primary sex education role models. Parents can lay a solid foundation for their child's understanding of sex and relationships by modeling healthy relationships, encouraging open communication, establishing limits, and engaging in safe sexual activity.

Therefore, spend some time discussing sex and relationships with your partner and your child, and serve as an example of the behaviors you wish to see in your child's future relationships.

Examining the impact parents have on their children's attitudes towards sex

Your attitudes and beliefs about sex as a parent can have a big impact on how your child feels about sex. Children look to their parents for direction and assistance from a young age, and this is particularly true when it comes to sex education.

Here are some strategies parents can use to influence how their kids feel about sex:

Positivity regarding sex: Children are more likely to have favorable attitudes toward sex and see it as a healthy and natural aspect of life when their parents do.

Children can have a healthy and good attitude toward sex with the assistance of parents who are open and honest about sex.

Negative sexual attitude: On the other side, parents who see sex negatively or as shameful or taboo may have a detrimental influence on their children's attitudes toward sex.

This may result in feelings of guilt, shame, or uncertainty towards relationships and sex.

Communication: How parents talk to their kids about sex might have an effect on how they feel about sex.

Children can develop a healthy and good attitude about sex with the assistance of parents who are open and honest about sex and who provide a safe and judgment-free environment for their children to ask questions.

Role modeling: Parents can significantly influence their children's attitudes regarding sex by setting an example of healthy and positive behaviors and attitudes toward sex.

Parents can assist their children in developing healthy and good attitudes toward sex by modeling healthy communication, mutual respect, and sex behavior.

Case Study: An open and accepting mother talked to her daughter about sex when the girl was quite young.

Her daughter as a result had a healthy and optimistic attitude toward sex and relationships. She felt comfortable discussing her sexual identity openly with her mother and was able to ask any questions she had.

Parents can assist their children in developing healthy and positive attitudes toward sex and relationships by adopting a positive and open attitude toward sex, being open and honest with their children, modeling healthy behaviors, and providing a safe and judgment-free environment for their children to ask questions.

Therefore, take the time to explore how your own views about sex may be influencing your child's views and ideas.

Ways to model healthy sexual behaviors and attitudes for your child

There are several important tactics you can employ when it comes to teaching your child healthy sexual attitudes and practices.

You can help your child develop a good and informed view on sex and relationships by modeling these behaviors and attitudes in your own life.

You can give your child the following examples of positive sexual behavior and attitudes:

Practice Communication: One of the most crucial things parents can do is to set a good example for their children when it comes to talking about sex and relationships.

This entails being straightforward and honest with your kid, responding to their inquiries in a mature and polite manner, and letting them express their own ideas and emotions.

You can help to establish a healthy environment for your child to learn and grow by demonstrating to them that talking about sex is a common and natural topic of conversation.

Demonstrate Consent: The value of consent in sexual relationships is another crucial conduct to exemplify.

In order to do this, you must teach your child that they should always ask their partners' consent before engaging in any sexual behavior and that they have the right to say "no" to any sexual activity that they find uncomfortable.

You can aid in fostering these qualities in your child by acting respectfully and consensually in your own relationships.

Stress Health and Safety: It's crucial to teach your youngster healthy and safe sexual conduct. This entails utilizing contraception to stop unwanted pregnancies and STDs, as well as scheduling routine exams and screenings to protect your sexual health.

You can help to stress the significance of healthy and educated sexual conduct by demonstrating to your child that sexual health is a priority.

This entails communicating your boundaries with your partner, acknowledging your own, and educating your children to do the same. You can aid your child in learning these skills by exhibiting appropriate boundaries and communication in your own interactions.

Your child can develop a positive and informed view on sex and relationships by observing your own healthy sexual actions and attitudes. Because your child imitates you, it's crucial to be aware of the messages you're conveying.

You may support your child's development into a responsible and respectful adult by placing a high priority on open communication, consent, health and safety, and healthy limits.

Common mistakes parents make when discussing sex education with their children

Talking about sex education can be a delicate and sometimes uncomfortable subject for parents to navigate.

As a result, some parents may inadvertently make mistakes that can negatively impact their child's understanding of sex and relationships. In this chapter, we will discuss some common mistakes parents make when discussing sex education with their children and provide tips on how to avoid them.

Mistake #1: Avoiding the conversation altogether

One of the most common mistakes parents make is avoiding the conversation altogether. While it may be uncomfortable to discuss sex and relationships with your child, it's important not to avoid the topic entirely. Your child will likely have questions and curiosity about these subjects, and if they don't get answers from you, they may seek out information from less reliable sources like their peers or the internet.

Tip: Start the conversation early and make it an ongoing dialogue. It's better to have small conversations over time than one big talk. Use everyday situations as opportunities to bring up the topic, like during a TV show or movie, or when a friend or family member is pregnant.

Mistake #2: Using fear tactics

Another mistake parents make is using fear tactics to discourage their child from engaging in sexual activity.

While it's important to educate your child about the risks associated with sex, using scare tactics can cause them to feel shame or anxiety about their own sexuality.

Tip: Focus on positive messages about healthy relationships and the importance of respecting oneself and one's partner. Talk openly and honestly about the potential consequences of sex, including STIs and pregnancy, but also emphasize the importance of communication and consent.

Mistake #3: Being too clinical

Some parents may feel uncomfortable discussing sex and relationships and as a result, may approach the conversation in a clinical or detached manner. This can make it difficult for your child to connect with the information you're presenting.

Tip: Use age-appropriate language and be open and honest with your child. Use examples and stories to help illustrate your points and make the conversation more relatable. Remember to be empathetic and understanding of your child's perspective.

Mistake #4: Not discussing LGBTQ+ issues

Many parents make the mistake of assuming their child is straight and therefore, may not address LGBTQ+ issues during sex education conversations. This can be damaging to LGBTQ+ youth who may feel excluded or unsupported.

Remember to bring up LGBTQ+ topics when talking about sex and relationships. Be welcoming and accepting of all gender identities and sexual orientations. Ask your youngster if they have any queries or worries regarding LGBTQ+ topics while using inclusive language.

The fifth error is giving false information.

When talking to their kids about sex education, parents frequently give erroneous information. This might be the result of ignorance or uneasiness with the topic.

Before talking to your youngster about sex and relationships, educate yourself on the subject. Be upfront about your knowledge and lack thereof, and don't be hesitant to acknowledge your inability to provide a solution. When in doubt, look it up jointly or receive advice from a dependable source.

Conclusion: Talking about sex education with your child might be difficult, but avoiding the topic or skipping crucial steps can have unfavorable effects. With your child, you may foster a healthy understanding of sex and relationships by being open, truthful, and sympathetic.

CHAPTER THREE

Understanding Your Child – Setting the Stage

It can be difficult for parents to comprehend their pre-teen children. They are starting to have their own thoughts, feelings, and views at this age, which may differ greatly from what you are used to hearing from them.

But it's important to take the time to comprehend your child's particular viewpoint, especially when it comes to sex education.

The fact that pre-teens are just beginning to traverse the world of puberty and sexuality is one of the most crucial things to keep in mind.

They could be perplexed or unsure about how their bodies are changing and how their sexual desires are developing. It is your responsibility as a parent to provide a welcoming, accepting environment where your children feel free to express their worries and ask questions.

Early trust-building and open communication are crucial for laying the groundwork for constructive discussion of sex education.

This entails being friendly and accessible, paying attention to your child's worries, and giving accurate information in a compassionate way.

Understanding your pre-teen's communication preferences and learning style is also essential. While some kids might benefit from visual assistance, others might prefer to read or hear information delivered logically and step-by-step.

You may make sure that your youngster is more open to the knowledge you're giving by adapting your approach to their particular learning style.

Realizing that your pre-teen may have a short attention span is essential to knowing them.

It's crucial to divide discussions about sex education into smaller, more digestible bits rather than dumping a ton of material on the subject at once.

They will be better able to retain what they are learning and make future judgments with more knowledge thanks to this.

Understanding your pre-teen child ultimately involves fostering a secure and encouraging environment where they feel at ease talking about sex education and asking questions.

You may help lay the groundwork for a healthy and informed understanding of sexuality by developing trust and open lines of communication, adapting your approach to their particular learning style, and structuring conversations into manageable pieces.

Changes that occur during puberty and how they impact your child's understanding of sex

Every child experiences puberty, which is a normal developmental period, but it can be a difficult time for both the child and the parent. Understanding the changes that take place throughout puberty and how they affect your child's perception of sex is crucial for parents.

First and foremost, it's crucial to have frank conversations with your child about how their bodies are changing.

This entails talking about both the possible mental changes, such as mood swings and heightened self-awareness, as well as the physical changes that will take place throughout puberty, such as breast development in girls and voice changes in boys.

You can make your child feel more at ease and confident as they traverse this time of life by setting the stage early on and explaining these developments in an age-appropriate way.

Children who are going through puberty frequently ask, "Why am I going through these changes?" It's crucial to convey to your child that these changes are a normal aspect of maturing and that they affect everyone differently and at various periods.

The fact that each person's body is unique and that there is no right or wrong method for their body to develop should also be emphasized.

The query "What is happening to me?" is another prevalent one. The changes they are going through may cause your child to feel confused or overwhelmed, so it's crucial to provide them correct information. Tell your child its okay to be inquisitive or worried about these changes, and encourage them to ask questions.

It's also crucial to teach your youngster the meaning of consent. They may start to feel arousal or sexual attraction as their body develops, and it's crucial for them to realize that they have control over their body and its changes. You may assist your child in developing healthy sexual attitudes and behaviors by teaching them the value of consent and respecting other people's boundaries.

Ultimately, you can help your child feel more confident and prepared as they traverse this crucial time of their development by recognizing the changes that happen during puberty and being open with them about these changes.

Here are effective steps to help you achieve this!

Start Early: It is important to start talking to your child about puberty and sex before they reach the age of 10. This way, they are better prepared for the changes that will occur in their bodies and have a solid foundation of knowledge to build upon.

Use Age-Appropriate Language: Use language that is appropriate for your child's age and level of understanding. This will ensure that they are able to follow the conversation and not feel overwhelmed or embarrassed.

Be Open and Honest: Be open and honest with your child about the changes that occur during puberty, including physical changes and hormonal changes. Explain that these changes are a normal part of growing up and that everyone goes through them.

Address Their Concerns: Take the time to listen to your child's concerns and answer their questions honestly. If you don't know the answer to a question, tell them that you will look it up and get back to them.

Provide Resources: Provide your child with resources such as books, websites, or videos that they can use to learn more about puberty and sex. This will give them the opportunity to explore the topic further on their own and in a way that is comfortable for them.

Encourage Communication: Encourage your child to come to you with any questions or concerns they may have. Let them know that they can always talk to you about anything and that you will be there to support them.

Be a Good Role Model: Model healthy attitudes and behaviors towards sex and relationships. This will help your child develop a positive attitude towards sex and relationships as they grow older.

Remember, the most important thing is to have an open and honest dialogue with your child. By doing so, you can help them understand the changes that occur during puberty and how they impact their understanding of sex in a healthy and positive way.

The importance of building a strong relationship with your child before having "the talk""

It can be intimidating to have "the talk" about sex with your child. You might experience awkwardness, embarrassment, or even be at a loss for words.

However, it's imperative that you have this conversation because it could have a big impact on your child's sexual health and wellbeing.

Prior to delving into the mechanics of sex education, it's critical to establish a solid rapport with your child based on open communication and trust. This is setting up a setting where your child feels safe and at ease discussing anything with you, even delicate subjects like sex.

Spending quality time with your child is one method to develop this kind of bond. It doesn't have to be anything elaborate or pricey; it might be as easy as playing board games or taking a stroll around the park.

You can convey to your child that they are important to you and that you are there to assist them by taking an interest in their lives and spending time with them.

Being a good listener to your child is another approach to develop a close bond with them. Always give your child your whole attention when they come to you with an issue or concern.

Try to understand things from their perspective and refrain from interrupting or ignoring their emotions. By doing this, you show them that you value their ideas and perspectives, which can assist to cement your relationship.

You can start bringing up sex education with your child if you've established a solid foundation of trust and open communication.

However, don't anticipate having "the talk" all at once; instead, proceed gradually and utilize teaching moments to initiate the discussion.

Use a sexually explicit scene in a TV show or movie you're viewing with your child as an opportunity to discuss healthy relationships and boundaries. Alternatively, use your child's inquiry about sex or their changing body as a starting point for a talk.

You may create the conditions for an honest and healthy discussion about sex by developing a strong bond with your child and introducing sex education gradually.

Negative outcomes, such as unwanted pregnancies, STIs, and toxic relationships, may be avoided as a result. Remember that having "the talk" takes continual communication and calls for trust, respect, and understanding.

Here is a case study to help you comprehend how this functions.

The Smiths are a family. Two children, a son, Jack, 12, and a daughter, Emily, 10, make up their family of four.

Both Emily and Jack are at the point where they are starting to wonder more about their bodies and sexuality. The Smiths want to build a good relationship with their kids first because they know how important it is for parents to have "the talk" with their children.

The Smiths have employed a few techniques to forge a solid bond with their children in order to accomplish this.

They first schedule time to spend with each child separately, engaging in things they both like. Jack might want to play video games or kick a ball around the backyard, whereas Emily would want to bake cookies or paint nails together.

This enables them to establish trust with their children and form bonds based on common interests.

Second, the Smiths always listen to their kids without passing judgment or offering constructive feedback. They encourage their children to express themselves, even when it is embarrassing or uncomfortable.

When talking about delicate subjects like sex education, it is critical that parents and children have an open and honest connection.

Thirdly, the Smiths foster a secure and encouraging atmosphere at home. They communicate to their kids that they are always available to them for advice and support and that they may turn to them with any inquiries or problems.

When the time comes for "the talk," the Smiths have already set the stage for a constructive dialogue.

Knowing that their parents would listen to them and offer advice without passing judgment, their kids feel safe and at ease enough to ask questions and express their opinions.

Here are some explanations on why it's crucial to build a solid bond with your child before having "the talk" regarding sex education:

Trust: When you have a strong relationship with your child, they are more likely to trust you and feel comfortable talking to you about sensitive topics like sex education. This can help prevent them from seeking misinformation from unreliable sources.

Open communication: A strong relationship with your child can also help create an environment of open communication. This means that they will feel more comfortable asking questions and seeking advice from you, rather than feeling embarrassed or ashamed.

Support: By building a strong relationship with your child, you can show them that you support and care for them. This can help them feel more confident and secure, which can be especially important during the confusing and often stressful time of puberty.

Positive role model: When you have a strong relationship with your child, you become a positive role model for them.

This means that they are more likely to emulate your behaviors and attitudes towards sex and relationships, which can have a positive impact on their own development.

By building a strong relationship with their children, the Smiths have set the stage for a successful sex education conversation. It's a win-win situation - their children feel supported and valued, while the parents have peace of mind knowing that their kids are equipped with the knowledge and tools they need to make safe and healthy choices.

Addressing common misconceptions about sex that tweens may have

It's crucial to dispel any misunderstandings your youngster may have about sex education. Peers, the media, and the internet frequently spread inaccurate information about sex to tweens, which can cause confusion and misunderstandings.

As a parent, it's imperative to dispel these myths and give your child real facts in a manner that they can grasp.

Tweens frequently believe that sex is solely about sexual pleasure, which is a widespread fallacy.

While sex does involve some element of physical pleasure, it's crucial to instill in your child the idea that sex also involves emotional intimacy and connection between two individuals.

The significance of consent, respect, and communication in any sexual experience must be emphasized.

Another widespread misunderstanding among tweens is that only heterosexual couples engage in sexual activity.

It's crucial to convey to your child that sex is possible for people of all sexual orientations and that attraction and affection are not gender-specific.

It's crucial to dispel the myth that having sex is always risk-free and without repercussions.

Your youngster has to be aware of the dangers associated with sexual activity, such as STDs and unwanted pregnancies. Teach your youngster the value of safety and responsible sex behavior.

Finally, some tweens could think that having sex is humiliating or disgusting.

It's crucial for parents to dispel this myth and teach their children that sex is a normal aspect of life and nothing to be embarrassed of.

Encourage your youngster to open up to you about their ideas and feelings regarding sex without worrying that you'll judge them.

It's imperative to address these widespread myths in order to give your child accurate and thorough sex education.

Giving your child accurate knowledge can enable them to make educated decisions and cultivate positive attitudes toward sex.

Here are some COMMON misconceptions your child may have

1. The myth that sex always leads to pregnancy: Many tweens believe that pregnancy is the inevitable outcome of any sexual encounter, which can cause anxiety and fear around sex.
2. The myth that only females can get pregnant: Many tweens are unaware of the biological processes involved in reproduction and may believe that only females can get pregnant.
3. The myth that using two condoms is safer than one: Tweens may believe that using two condoms during sex provides extra protection against STIs and pregnancy, but in reality, using two condoms can actually increase the risk of breakage and decrease effectiveness.
4. The myth that you can't get an STI from oral sex: Tweens may believe that oral sex is completely safe and cannot lead to STIs, but the reality is that many STIs can be transmitted through oral sex.
5. The myth that everyone is having sex: Many tweens may feel pressure to engage in sexual activity because they

believe that everyone else is doing it. This can lead to feelings of isolation and anxiety.

Here are answers to the Misconceptions

1. Misconception: Everyone is having sex, and it's cool to do so. Response: Explain that while sex may seem like a big deal at their age, it's important to wait until they are ready and in a healthy, consensual relationship. Help them understand that not everyone is having sex, and that there's nothing wrong with waiting.
2. Misconception: Condoms aren't necessary or don't work well. Response: Explain that condoms are an important part of preventing unintended pregnancies and sexually transmitted infections (STIs). Help your child understand how to properly use condoms and emphasize that they are effective when used correctly.
3. Misconception: Birth control pills protect against STIs. Response: Explain that birth control pills are meant to prevent pregnancy, but they do not protect against STIs. Encourage your child to use condoms in addition to other forms of birth control.
4. Misconception: Masturbation is wrong or dirty. Response: Explain that masturbation is a normal and healthy part of sexual development. Let your child know that it's okay to explore their body and that it's important to do so in a private setting.
5. Misconception: Only girls can get pregnant. Response: Explain that both boys and girls have a role in pregnancy. Emphasize that it takes a sperm from a boy and an egg

from a girl to create a pregnancy, and that both partners need to take responsibility for their actions.

It's important to approach these conversations with sensitivity and empathy, and to create a safe space for your child to ask questions and express their thoughts and feelings.

Providing accurate information and debunking common misconceptions can help your child develop a healthy and positive attitude towards sex.

CHAPTER FOUR

Beginning the Conversation about Sex, Body and Relationships

Talking to your child about their changing bodies, the idea of sex, and romantic relationships is crucial as they get closer to puberty.

However, having this talk with your child can be challenging and overwhelming for both of you. Herein lies the significance of starting the conversation.

Setting the stage for future discussions and fostering in your child a positive attitude toward their sexuality is possible by starting the conversation about the body, sex, and relationships.

In this chapter, we'll look at how to start this conversation with your kid in a way that's enjoyable for both of you, educational, and comfortable.

Find a natural opening in the conversation as a starting point. Use a show or movie you're watching—for instance, one about sex or relationships—as a springboard to strike up a conversation.

Asking your child about the subject will allow you to learn more about how they feel about it and whether they have any questions.

Another strategy is to create a cozy atmosphere. You may do this by having a conversation with your child while sitting down in a private section of the house, such as their room.

You might also think about having the discussion when the two of you are doing something else, like taking a walk or doing a problem. Your child is more likely to feel at ease and open up if you foster a calm environment.

Additionally, it's critical to be upfront and honest with your youngster. This entails speaking in a way that is acceptable for their age and giving honest responses.

Don't be afraid to bring up challenging or uncomfortable subjects. Instead, provide your youngster knowledge that is honest, truthful, and easy to understand.

Additionally useful for starting the conversation are examples. To explain the subject you're talking about, for instance, you could utilize a case study or tale. This can help your youngster relate to the subject and comprehend it better.

Finally, always keep patience and understanding in mind. Your child can have numerous inquiries or might experience awkwardness or embarrassment while listening to the dialogue.

Be ready to respond to their inquiries and concerns in a considerate and encouraging manner.

By using these suggestions, you can start a conversation with your child about the body, sex, and relationships in a way that is enjoyable and comfortable for both of you. By doing so, you may help your child form a healthy and accepting attitude toward their sexuality and build the framework for future conversations.

You can always use the following sample format to start a conversation with your child:

Let's imagine that when your youngster is watching their favorite TV program, a kissing scene occurs between two characters. You should take advantage of this chance to bring up boundaries and relationships.

Say something along the lines of, "Hey, did you witness that kissing scene? How did you feel about it? This may encourage your youngster to talk about romantic relationships and to discuss their sentiments.

You can then move on to a more detailed discussion of boundaries, consent, and healthy relationships. To make it relatable and enjoyable, use examples from your child's favorite TV episodes or movies.

You may, for instance, ask your youngster if they have ever seen a television or movie character who didn't respect their partner's boundaries.

What impression do you believe that gave the other person? Your youngster will learn the value of respecting others and establishing boundaries in their personal interactions as a result of this.

You may have a conversation with your child that is more interesting and pertinent to their interests by sharing examples from media that they appreciate.

FOR BOYS

- Bring up a situation that happened to a friend or a family member and ask them what they think about it. For example, "I heard that your friend's sister got pregnant in high school. What do you think about that?" This can open up a discussion about the consequences of having sex and the importance of being responsible.
- Use humor to lighten the mood. For example, "Hey, did you hear about the birds and the bees? Let's talk about it." This can help to reduce tension and make the conversation less awkward.
- Start with basic anatomy. For example, "Hey, did you know that boys have a penis and girls have a vagina?" This can help to build a foundation for further discussions about sex and relationships.

FOR GIRLS

- Bring up a current event related to relationships or sex, such as a news story or a celebrity scandal, and ask them what they think about it. For example, "What do you think about the recent scandal with (insert celebrity name)?"
- Use a book or a movie as a jumping-off point for discussion. For example, if you're reading a book together that includes a romantic subplot, you could ask them what they think about the characters' relationship.
- Start with basic anatomy. For example, "Hey, did you know that girls have a uterus and boys don't?" This can help to build a foundation for further discussions about sex and relationships.

Remember, every child is different, and what works for one child may not work for another. The key is to keep an open mind, be non-judgmental, and approach the conversation with empathy and understanding.

Discussing the best ways to start the conversation with your child

It's crucial to establish an atmosphere of transparency and trust first and foremost. Tell your child that you will support them and provide any questions they may have without passing judgment or feeling ashamed.

It's crucial to get the dialogue going without passing judgment or offering criticism. Say something along the lines of, "I want to talk to you about something that can be difficult, but I want you to know that I'm here to listen and help you."

Making use of teaching opportunities is a further excellent strategy.

Consider using a sex scene in a movie or TV show as an occasion to discuss it with your child and share your own opinions. Or, take advantage of the chance to bring up safe sex and healthy relationships if a friend or family member gets married or pregnant.

Adapting the talk to your child's age and developmental stage is also crucial.

Use age-appropriate language and concentrate on teaching the fundamentals of anatomy and consent to younger children. For older kids, you can delve more deeply into subjects like birth control, STDs, and healthy relationships.

It's crucial to underline that the dialogue is continuing and that you are always open for discourse. Encourage any queries or worries your child may have to come to you, and be ready to bring up the subject again as they mature and their understanding of sexuality changes.

In order to help your child have a healthy and happy connection with their sexuality, remember that having "the talk" with them is a crucial first step. It may be a gratifying experience for you and your child if you take the appropriate approach.

Addressing common questions your child may have about sex and relationships

Can I get pregnant or get someone pregnant from kissing? Answer: No, pregnancy can only occur when sperm from a male partner fertilizes an egg from a female partner. This can only happen during sexual intercourse.

Is it okay to have sex with someone who is much older than me? Answer: It is important to have sex only when you are ready and with someone you trust and feel comfortable with. It is not okay for someone who is much older to pressure or force you into having sex.

What is the difference between love and lust? Answer: Love is a deep feeling of affection and care for someone, while lust is a strong desire or craving for sexual pleasure. It is important to understand the difference between the two and to engage in sexual activities only when they are accompanied by love and respect.

What is a healthy relationship? Answer: A healthy relationship is one where both partners communicate openly and honestly, respect each other's boundaries and choices, and feel supported and cared for by their partner. It is important to have a healthy relationship to ensure that both partners feel safe, secure, and happy.

What is consent? Answer: Consent is when all parties involved in a sexual activity agree to participate in it freely and without pressure or coercion. It is important to always obtain consent before engaging in any sexual activity.

Is it okay to have sex before marriage? Answer: The decision to have sex before marriage is a personal one that varies from person to person and is influenced by factors such as culture, religion, and personal beliefs. It is important to understand the risks and consequences associated with engaging in sexual activity, and to always engage in it safely and consensually.

It is important to note that sexual activity and relationships are a natural part of human development and should not be entirely avoided or stigmatized. Parents may want to delay their child's sexual debut until they are ready to engage in a safe, consensual, and healthy sexual relationship. Here are some measures that parents can take to help their child delay sexual activity and relationships:

Encourage open communication: Create a safe space where your child feels comfortable talking about sexual activity and relationships. Encourage them to ask questions, express their feelings, and share their concerns.

Educate your child: Provide your child with comprehensive and age-appropriate sex education. This should include information about anatomy, puberty, relationships, consent, contraception, and sexually transmitted infections.

Set clear boundaries and expectations: Discuss your values, beliefs, and expectations about sex and relationships with your child. Set clear rules and consequences for breaking them.

Monitor your child's activities: Keep an eye on your child's activities both in-person and online. Know who their friends are, where they go, and what they do. Monitor their social media and internet use.

Encourage healthy relationships: Teach your child about healthy relationships that are based on mutual respect, communication, and trust. Encourage them to seek out positive role models and surround themselves with friends who share similar values.

Build self-esteem: Help your child build self-esteem and confidence by praising their achievements, encouraging their interests, and supporting their goals.

Be a good role model: Model healthy and respectful behaviors in your own relationships. Your child learns from your actions and words, so make sure you're setting a good example.

Remember, these measures are not foolproof, but they can help reduce the likelihood of your child engaging in sexual activity or relationships before they are ready.

Here are some more detailed explanations on the steps parents can take to help their children abstain from sex and relationships until they are ready:

Open communication: Talking openly and honestly with your child about sex and relationships is essential. Discussing the potential risks and consequences of engaging in sexual activity before they are ready can help them make informed decisions. It is important to listen to their concerns and address any questions they may have.

Teach healthy boundaries: Help your child understand what healthy boundaries are and how to establish them in relationships. Encourage them to speak up and say no when someone is pressuring them into something they are uncomfortable with.

Set rules and guidelines: Establish clear rules and guidelines for your child's behavior, such as curfews, appropriate attire, and rules around internet and social media usage. Consistently enforcing these rules will help your child understand the importance of self-discipline and self-control.

Provide alternatives: Encourage your child to participate in activities that don't involve romantic relationships or sexual activity. This could include sports, hobbies, volunteering, or spending time with friends and family.

Build self-esteem: Helping your child build a strong sense of self-worth and confidence can go a long way in helping them resist peer pressure and make healthy decisions. Praise their accomplishments, encourage their interests, and be supportive and loving.

Be a positive role model: Your behavior and attitudes towards relationships and sex can have a significant impact on your child's beliefs and actions. Be a positive role model by exhibiting healthy behaviors and attitudes, such as setting boundaries and communicating openly with your partner.

Remember, it's important to have ongoing conversations with your child about sex and relationships, as attitudes and behaviors can change over time.

By taking an active role in their lives and being a positive influence, you can help your child make informed decisions and develop healthy attitudes towards sex and relationships.

Providing age-appropriate information and resources for your child to learn more

To help your child learn more about sex and relationships, as a parent, you should give them age-appropriate knowledge and tools. As they get older, this will help them make wise judgments.

Giving kids books or other materials made for their age group is one approach to achieve this. For instance, you might offer books that explain the distinctions between boys and girls to younger children and books that cover more sophisticated subjects like consent and healthy relationships to older children.

Additionally, you can benefit from online tools like films and webpages created especially for kids and teenagers. Many of these tools are interactive and may make learning interesting and fun for your kid.

Additionally, you can provide your child the chance to speak with dependable adults, such teachers, coaches, or counselors, who can give them correct information and nonjudgmental answers to their questions.

Overall, helping your child develop a healthy perspective of sex and relationships involves giving them with resources and information that are age-appropriate. Additionally, it can make individuals feel more at ease and certain while they deal with these issues.

CHAPTER FIVE

How Much Talk can be Too Much

Talking to your child about sex is important, but how much is too much?

At what point do you cross the line from providing valuable information to overwhelming your child with too much detail? These are valid concerns for parents to consider when discussing the nitty-gritty of sex education.

One important thing to keep in mind is that children have different levels of maturity and comfort when it comes to discussing sex.

Some children may be more curious and ask more questions, while others may feel embarrassed or uncomfortable. As a parent, it's your job to gauge your child's level of comfort and adjust your approach accordingly.

One effective strategy is to provide information in small, manageable doses. Instead of overwhelming your child with all the details of sex and relationships at once, break the information down into smaller, age-appropriate chunks.

For example, when discussing puberty with a young child, you might start with the basics of bodily changes before moving on to more detailed information about sex and relationships as they grow older.

It's also important to create an environment where your child feels comfortable asking questions and expressing their feelings.

Encourage an open dialogue by being approachable and non-judgmental. Let your child know that they can come to you with any questions or concerns, and that you are there to provide support and guidance.

Using everyday situations as opportunities to teach your child can also be effective.

For example, when watching a movie or TV show with your child that includes a romantic relationship or sex scene, use it as a starting point to discuss the emotions and consequences involved.

This allows your child to learn in a more natural and relatable way, rather than feeling like they are being lectured.

Another helpful tip is to provide resources for your child to learn more on their own. This can include books, articles, websites, and other media that provide accurate and age-appropriate information.

You can also point them towards trusted organizations that provide sex education resources, such as Planned Parenthood or Advocates for Youth.

It's important to find a balance when discussing sensitive topics such as sex and relationships with your child.

Too little information can leave them confused and uninformed, while too much information can be overwhelming and even inappropriate for their age and developmental stage. Here are some tips to help you strike the right balance:

Consider your child's age and developmental stage: It's important to provide age-appropriate information to your child. A young child may not need to know as much as a teenager. You can start by discussing basic concepts such as body parts and boundaries with younger children and gradually introduce more complex topics as they grow older.

Listen to your child: Encourage your child to ask questions and listen carefully to what they have to say. This will help you understand their level of understanding and adjust your conversation accordingly.

Keep it simple: Avoid using complex language or overwhelming your child with too much information at once. Use simple words and phrases that they can easily understand.

Provide information gradually: Break down information into small chunks and provide it gradually over time. This will help your child digest the information and prevent them from feeling overwhelmed.

Avoid oversharing: Be mindful of the amount of personal information you share with your child. While it's important to be honest, it's also important to maintain appropriate boundaries and not overshare.

Be honest: It's important to be honest with your child, but also to know when to hold back. If you don't know the answer to a question or feel uncomfortable discussing a certain topic, it's okay to say so.

Discussing the nitty-gritty of sex education can be a delicate balance, but with the right approach, it can be done effectively.

Providing information in small, manageable doses, creating an open and approachable environment, using everyday situations as teachable moments, and providing resources for your child to learn more on their own are all strategies that can help ensure your child receives the information they need in a way that is age-appropriate and effective.

In the context of discussing sex and relationships, the term "nitty-gritty" refers to the specific details of sexual anatomy, sexual behavior, contraception, and the potential consequences of sexual activity.

These topics can be sensitive and complex, and require a delicate approach when discussing them with children or teenagers.

When talking to children about sex, it's important to remember that they may not have a full understanding of the various concepts and terminology involved.

Therefore, parents should approach the topic with sensitivity and provide information in a way that is age-appropriate and understandable for their child.

The nitty-gritty details of sex education can vary depending on the age of the child, their level of curiosity, and their individual level of knowledge.

For younger children, the focus may be more on basic concepts like the differences between boys and girls, or the idea of "private parts." For older children and teenagers, the discussion may include more complex topics like sexual health, contraception, and consent.

Ultimately, the goal of discussing the nitty-gritty of sex education with children is to provide them with accurate information and empower them to make informed decisions about their sexual health and relationships as they grow older.

By approaching the topic with sensitivity and an age-appropriate approach, parents can help their children feel comfortable and confident when discussing these important topics.

Best ways to answer your child's questions without overwhelming your kids

Here are some additional techniques that can be used when answering your child's questions without overwhelming them:

- Use analogies and metaphors: Sometimes, explaining a concept using a familiar analogy or metaphor can help make it more understandable and less overwhelming. For example, you might use an analogy like "sex is like putting together a puzzle, where the pieces only fit together in a certain way" to explain the importance of consent and respecting boundaries.
- Break down complex concepts: If your child asks a question that relates to a complex concept, it can be helpful to break it down into smaller parts. For example, if your child asks about the biological process of reproduction, you might start by explaining how a sperm and an egg

combine to form a zygote, before moving on to the different stages of fetal development.
- Encourage your child to ask follow-up questions: It's important to let your child take the lead in these conversations and encourage them to ask follow-up questions if there's something they don't understand. This can help ensure that they're only getting information that they're ready for and that they can process in a healthy way.
- Use age-appropriate language: It's important to use language that is appropriate for your child's age and level of understanding. This can help ensure that they're not overwhelmed by information that is too complex for them to process.
- **Validate your child's feelings:** Sometimes, questions about sex and relationships can bring up uncomfortable or difficult emotions for your child. It's important to validate these feelings and let your child know that it's okay to feel this way. This can help them feel more comfortable and less overwhelmed during these conversations.

Parents can ensure that they are answering their child's questions in a way that is informative and supportive without being overwhelming.

How to provide accurate information without being too explicit

Trust me providing accurate information without being too explicit can be a tricky balance to strike. One approach that can be helpful is to use age-appropriate language and avoid overly graphic or technical terms. For example, instead of using medical terms like "vagina" or "penis," you might use more accessible terms like "private parts" or "down there."

Another helpful tip is to let your child guide the conversation and respond to their questions in a way that is direct and honest, but still age-appropriate.

This might mean simplifying complex concepts or using metaphors or analogies to help them understand. For example, you might compare the reproductive system to a car engine or a plant's reproductive organs.

It's also important to establish boundaries and ground rules for the conversation.

Let your child know that they can ask questions, but that certain topics may be off-limits or reserved for discussion at a later time. This can help to prevent them from feeling overwhelmed or uncomfortable during the conversation.

Additionally, it can be helpful to provide your child with resources or books that they can read on their own to learn more about sex and relationships.

This can give them the opportunity to explore these topics at their own pace and in a way that feels comfortable for them.

Remember, the key is to provide accurate information in a way that is appropriate for your child's age and developmental stage.

By striking this balance, you can help your child develop a healthy and informed understanding of sex and relationships.

Addressing common concerns parents have about discussing sensitive topics with their children

Talking to children about sensitive topics can be a daunting task for many parents.

However, it is an important conversation that parents should have with their children to ensure that they are informed and prepared to make healthy decisions.

As a parent, it's common to have concerns and fears about discussing sensitive topics such as sex, relationships, and personal safety with your child.

In this article, we will explore some of the most common concerns that parents have and provide practical solutions for addressing them.

Fear of providing too much information: One of the most common concerns that parents have is the fear of giving too much information to their child.

It's important to remember that the level of information you provide should be age-appropriate and relevant to your child's understanding.

For example, a young child may not need to know about the specifics of sexual intercourse, but it's important to teach them about personal boundaries and respect.

Fear of not knowing enough: Many parents worry that they don't have enough knowledge to talk to their child about sensitive topics. However, it's okay to admit that you don't know everything. If you're not sure about a question, it's better to say "I don't know, but let's find out together" than to give incorrect information.

Fear of being judged: Some parents may worry about being judged by their child for their own experiences or beliefs.

It's important to remember that the conversation should be about your child and their needs, not about you. Your job as a parent is to provide accurate information and support your child's development.

Fear of damaging the parent-child relationship: Parents may also worry that discussing sensitive topics with their child may damage their relationship.

However, research shows that talking to your child about sensitive topics can actually strengthen your relationship and increase trust. Your child will feel more comfortable coming to you with questions and concerns in the future.

To address these concerns, it's important to approach the conversation with an open and non-judgmental attitude.

Make sure you are in a comfortable and private setting and that you are giving your child your full attention.

Encourage your child to ask questions and listen to their concerns. Provide accurate and age-appropriate information and avoid using slang or euphemisms.

Remember that the conversation is a continuous process and not a one-time event. Be open to having ongoing conversations with your child as they grow and develop.

Discussing sensitive topics with your child can be a challenging task, but it's important to provide accurate information to ensure that your child is informed and prepared to make healthy decisions.

By addressing common concerns and taking a thoughtful approach, you can have a successful conversation with your child that strengthens your relationship and increases trust.

CHAPTER SIX

The Influence of the Media and What You Can Do About It

Are you concerned about the media's influence on your child's views on sex and relationships? You're not alone.

With the prevalence of social media, TV shows, movies, and other forms of media, it's important to consider the messages your child is receiving and how they might be shaping their beliefs and behaviors.

One way to address the media's influence is to have open and honest conversations with your child about what they're watching or reading. Encourage them to ask questions and express their thoughts and opinions.

By engaging in dialogue, you can help them develop critical thinking skills and make sense of the messages they're receiving.

It's also important to monitor your child's media consumption and set appropriate boundaries.

This can include limiting screen time, restricting access to certain types of media, or even watching shows or movies together so you can discuss any issues or concerns that arise.

Another way to counteract negative media messages is to provide your child with positive role models and resources.

Look for books, movies, and TV shows that promote healthy relationships, respect, and consent.

You can also encourage your child to seek out educational resources, such as websites or books that provide accurate information about sex and relationships.

Remember, as a parent, you have the power to shape your child's views and beliefs. By being proactive and involved in your child's media consumption, you can help them navigate the often confusing and contradictory messages they receive from the media.

Let's talk about the ways in which kids can be affected by the media, and the types of media channels that may have the biggest influence on them.

Children today are exposed to a vast array of media channels, including TV shows, movies, social media platforms, video games, and more.

These various media channels can have a significant impact on children, particularly in terms of their attitudes, beliefs, and behaviors related to sex and relationships.

For example, TV shows and movies often depict romantic relationships and sexual activity, and kids who watch these shows can be influenced by what they see.

Studies have found that exposure to sexual content in the media can lead to earlier sexual activity, more sexual partners, and decreased use of contraception among young people.

Social media is another platform that can have a significant influence on kids. Social media sites like Instagram, Snapchat, and TikTok are popular among young people and are often used to share sexualized content. This content can lead to unrealistic expectations about sex and relationships, and can also contribute to body image issues.

Video games are another form of media that can have an impact on children.

Many video games contain sexual content or portray sexual relationships, and research has found that exposure to sexual content in video games can increase the likelihood of engaging in risky sexual behaviors.

As a parent, it's important to be aware of the media channels that your child is exposed to, and to talk with them about the content they are seeing.

By having open and honest conversations with your child, you can help them to develop a healthy understanding of sex and relationships, and can guide them in making informed decisions about their own sexual behaviors.

The impact of media on tweens' understanding of sex and relationships

In today's digital age, the media is more present than ever, and it has a profound impact on how tweens perceive sex and relationships.

It's no secret that television shows, movies, and social media platforms often portray sex and relationships in unrealistic and often harmful ways. As a parent, it's essential to understand how the media can influence your child's understanding of sex and relationships, and what you can do to mitigate its negative effects.

One way that the media can affect tweens' understanding of sex and relationships is by portraying unrealistic and unhealthy relationship dynamics.

Many TV shows and movies romanticize possessiveness and jealousy, making it seem like these are normal and desirable traits in a relationship.

Social media can also perpetuate unrealistic relationship standards by presenting only the highlights of couples' lives and relationships, giving tweens a skewed perspective of what a healthy relationship looks like.

Moreover, media can also expose tweens to sexual content at an early age. Children are now exposed to a wide range of sexually explicit content on TV, movies, and social media.

They can come across pornography accidentally, leading to premature sexualization, and they might believe that what they see is normal behavior in real life.

As a parent, it's important to address these concerns and take steps to mitigate the negative effects of media on your tween's understanding of sex and relationships.

One of the most effective ways is to talk to your child about the content they're consuming and how it can affect their beliefs and attitudes towards sex and relationships. Discussing what's healthy and unhealthy in a relationship can help them discern what they see in the media.

Another way to mitigate the impact of media is to limit your child's exposure to sexually explicit content.

Monitor what they're watching on TV, what movies they're allowed to watch, and set parental controls on their social media accounts.

It's also important to engage your child in activities that promote positive values and healthy habits, such as sports, art, music, and community service.

Finally, leading by example can go a long way. As a parent, you can model healthy relationship behaviors, such as mutual respect, communication, and setting boundaries.

You can also monitor your own media consumption and show your child that you're critical of media's portrayal of sex and relationships.

The media has a significant impact on tweens' understanding of sex and relationships.

As a parent, it's important to be aware of how media can influence your child and take steps to mitigate its negative effects.

By having open and honest conversations, setting boundaries, and leading by example, you can help your child develop a healthy and realistic understanding of sex and relationships.

Addressing common stereotypes and misconceptions perpetuated by the media

As a parent or caregiver, it can be challenging to navigate the influence of media on tweens' understanding of sex and relationships. With so much information out there, it's important to address common misconceptions and stereotypes perpetuated by the media.

To get started, let's explore some common questions and answers regarding the impact of media on tweens:

Q: How does media influence tweens' understanding of sex and relationships?

A: Media can heavily influence tweens' understanding of sex and relationships by presenting unrealistic expectations, promoting harmful stereotypes, and normalizing risky behaviors.

For example, TV shows and movies may portray unrealistic and unhealthy relationship dynamics, while music videos may sexualize women and promote a culture of objectification.

Q: What are some media channels that may affect tweens' understanding of sex and relationships?

A: Some media channels that may influence tweens' understanding of sex and relationships include social media platforms like Instagram and TikTok, TV shows and movies, music videos, and even video games.

Q: What are some common stereotypes and misconceptions perpetuated by the media?

A: Some common stereotypes and misconceptions include the idea that boys should be sexually aggressive and girls should be passive, the belief that sex is always perfect and enjoyable for everyone involved, and the normalization of risky sexual behaviors like unprotected sex and alcohol use.

Now that we've explored some common questions and answers, let's dive deeper into addressing these stereotypes and misconceptions. Here are some examples of how you can approach these conversations with your tweens:

When watching a TV show or movie with your tween, use it as an opportunity to discuss the healthy and unhealthy relationship dynamics portrayed. Ask your tween how they feel about the relationships and whether they think they are healthy or not.

If you notice a music video or social media post that promotes harmful stereotypes or risky behaviors, talk to your tween about why it's problematic and how it can negatively impact their understanding of sex and relationships.

Use real-life examples from your own experiences or those of people you know to highlight the differences between reality and the media's portrayal of sex and relationships.

This can help your tween understand that what they see on TV or social media is not always an accurate representation of real life.

Overall, it's important to have open and honest conversations with your tweens about the impact of media on their understanding of sex and relationships. By providing accurate information, addressing common stereotypes and misconceptions, and using real-life examples, you can help your tweens develop a healthy and realistic understanding of these topics.

Providing strategies for helping your child navigate media messages about sex and relationships
Navigating media messages about sex and relationships can be tricky for parents and their children.

With so many sources of information available, it can be difficult to know what messages are accurate and appropriate for your child's age and maturity level.

Here are some strategies for helping your child navigate media messages about sex and relationships:

Start the conversation: One of the best things you can do to help your child navigate media messages about sex and relationships is to start the conversation early.

Talking to your child openly and honestly about sex and relationships, you can help them develop a healthy and informed perspective that can serve them well as they navigate the media landscape.

Monitor your child's media consumption: Monitoring your child's media consumption is another key strategy for helping them navigate media messages about sex and relationships.

By keeping tabs on what your child is watching, reading, and listening to, you can identify potential sources of misinformation or inappropriate content, and help your child develop the critical thinking skills needed to evaluate media messages for themselves.

Encourage critical thinking: Encouraging critical thinking is another important strategy for helping your child navigate media messages about sex and relationships.

By helping your child question the messages they receive from the media, you can help them develop the skills they need to think critically about the world around them.

Ask them questions like "What do you think about that message?" or "Do you think that message is accurate?" This will help them develop their own opinions and challenge any misinformation.

Provide accurate information: It is important to provide your child with accurate information about sex and relationships.

This can help them make informed decisions about their own lives and relationships, and can help them filter out inaccurate or harmful media messages.

Use media as a teaching tool: The media can also be used as a teaching tool.

By using movies, TV shows, and other media as a starting point for conversations about sex and relationships, you can help your child develop critical thinking skills and learn more about healthy relationships.

Here are some examples of how to use media as a teaching tool:

Watch a TV show or movie with your child and ask them questions about the characters' relationships and behaviors.

Use a news article or social media post as a starting point for a conversation about healthy relationships and boundaries.

Discuss how advertising and marketing messages can influence our perceptions of sex and relationships.

By using these strategies and examples, you can help your child navigate media messages about sex and relationships and develop a healthy and informed perspective on these important topics.

CHAPTER SEVEN

Sexual Safety and Self-Protection

When it comes to self-protection and sexual safety, there are many important factors to consider. As a parent, you want to do everything you can to help your child stay safe and make informed decisions about their sexual health.

Here are some strategies you can use to promote self-protection and sexual safety:

Teach your child about healthy boundaries and how to say no: Encourage your child to establish and respect personal boundaries, and to communicate their needs and limits clearly to others. Help them practice assertive communication so they can confidently say no when they need to.

Encourage your child to trust their instincts: Teach your child to listen to their inner voice and pay attention to warning signs or red flags when interacting with others. If something feels wrong or uncomfortable, they should know that it's okay to trust their instincts and remove themselves from the situation.

Model healthy relationships: Children learn a lot by watching the behavior of the adults around them. If you model healthy relationships with good communication, respect, and boundaries, your child is more likely to develop those same skills and habits.

Discuss the dangers of substance use: Substance use can impair judgment and decision-making, making it more difficult to stay safe in sexual situations. Talk to your child about the dangers of drug and alcohol use, and encourage them to avoid these substances altogether.

Teach your child to practice safe sex: If your child is sexually active, it's important to talk to them about safe sex practices such as using condoms and getting regular STI testing. Encourage them to prioritize their sexual health and to make informed decisions about their sexual activity.

Monitor your child's online activity: The internet can be a risky place for young people, with the potential for exposure to inappropriate content, predators, and cyberbullying. Stay involved in your child's online activity and use parental controls to limit their access to inappropriate content.

Encourage your child to report any concerning behavior: Teach your child that they can come to you or another trusted adult if they experience any concerning behavior or are made to feel uncomfortable in any way. Let them know that they won't be in trouble for reporting and that their safety is your top priority.

By following these strategies, you can help your child stay safe and make healthy decisions in sexual situations.

Discussing the importance of consent and healthy boundaries
Consent and healthy boundaries are essential topics to discuss with your child when it comes to sex and relationships. These conversations are not just important to prevent sexual violence and harassment but also to promote healthy relationships.

It's crucial for children to understand that consent is a crucial aspect of any sexual activity. Children should learn that they should never engage in any sexual activity without the explicit and enthusiastic consent of their partner. This understanding starts with setting healthy boundaries and learning to respect those of others.

Here are some strategies to discuss the importance of consent and healthy boundaries with your child:

Define what consent and healthy boundaries mean: It's important to explain these terms to your child in a clear and concise way. Define consent as the enthusiastic and mutual agreement between both partners before any sexual activity.

Help them understand that healthy boundaries mean respecting each other's limits and feelings.

Talk about what consent looks like: Use scenarios to illustrate what consent looks like in practice. For example, explain how it is important to obtain explicit verbal consent from a partner before any sexual activity.

Encourage your child to communicate: Encourage your child to communicate their boundaries and to ask their partner about their own. Teach them to listen actively and respectfully to their partner's responses and to respect their limits.

Discuss how consent can change: Explain to your child that consent can change throughout a sexual encounter. They should know that they can stop or change their mind at any time during sexual activity, and their partner must respect their decision.

Model healthy boundaries and respect: Children learn by example, so it's important to model healthy boundaries and respect in your own relationships. Talk openly with your child about how you and your partner communicate and respect each other's boundaries.

Here's an example scenario to explain the importance of consent and healthy boundaries:

Imagine your teenage daughter goes to a party with her friends. She meets a boy there who she thinks is cute and they start talking.

After a few minutes, the boy leans in to kiss her. Your daughter isn't sure if she wants to kiss him back, but she doesn't want to seem rude or hurt his feelings.

In this scenario, it's important for your daughter to understand that she has the right to say no, even if it might disappoint the boy.

By establishing healthy boundaries and understanding the importance of consent, she can protect herself from potentially uncomfortable or harmful situations.

If your daughter is unsure how to communicate her boundaries, you could suggest that she uses "I statements" to express herself clearly and directly. For example, she could say "I'm not comfortable with that" or "I don't want to do that."

By using assertive communication, she can make it clear that her boundaries are important and deserving of respect.

Remember, it's never too early to start teaching your child about consent and healthy boundaries. By having these important conversations and providing them with the tools to protect themselves, you can help your child develop healthy relationships and prevent harmful situations.

Discussing the importance of consent and healthy boundaries
In today's digital age, it is crucial to teach your child how to stay safe both online and in-person.

With so many different ways to communicate and interact with others, it's important to provide your child with strategies to protect themselves and their personal information. Here are some tips to help your child stay safe online and in-person:

Teach your child about online privacy: Discuss with your child the importance of keeping their personal information safe online.

Teach them to never give out their full name, address, phone number, or any other personal details online without your permission.

Set boundaries: Encourage your child to set boundaries both online and in-person. Teach them to say "no" if someone makes them feel uncomfortable or if they don't want to do something. Discuss with them the importance of trusting their instincts and speaking up if something doesn't feel right.

Monitor their online activity: Keep an eye on your child's online activity and monitor who they are communicating with. Discuss with them the importance of being cautious when talking to strangers online and remind them to never agree to meet someone in-person without your permission.

Use privacy settings: Make sure your child knows how to use privacy settings on social media and other online platforms. Teach them to only accept friend requests from people they know in real life and to always think twice before posting anything online.

Create a safety plan: Work with your child to create a safety plan for both online and in-person interactions. This could include setting rules for communicating with strangers online or establishing a code word or signal to use if they feel uncomfortable or unsafe.

Discuss safe sex practices: If your child is old enough to be exploring sexual relationships, it is important to have open and honest conversations with them about safe sex practices. Teach them about contraception and how to protect themselves from sexually transmitted infections.

Common concerns parents have about their child's safety

As a parent, your child's safety is your top priority. However, sometimes it can feel overwhelming and even scary to think about all the potential risks that could harm your child.

It's normal to have concerns, but it's important not to let fear dictate your actions. Here are some common concerns parents have about their child's safety and strategies for addressing them:

Stranger danger: Many parents worry about their child being abducted or harmed by a stranger. While these concerns are valid, it's important to remember that the majority of child abductions are committed by someone the child knows, such as a family member or acquaintance. Teach your child to recognize and trust their instincts, and to say "no" and get away from anyone who makes them uncomfortable.

Bullying: Bullying is a prevalent issue that can have serious consequences for children's mental health and well-being. Encourage your child to speak up if they or someone they know is being bullied. Teach them how to be assertive, but not aggressive, in standing up for themselves.

Internet safety: The internet can be a wonderful resource for children, but it also presents numerous risks. Make sure your child understands the importance of keeping personal information private and being cautious when interacting with strangers online. Set clear rules and boundaries for internet use, and consider using parental controls and monitoring software.

Accidents: Accidents can happen anywhere and anytime, but there are steps you can take to minimize the risks. Teach your child about basic safety practices, such as wearing helmets while biking, looking both ways before crossing the street, and staying away from potentially dangerous objects.

Substance abuse: Drug and alcohol use among teenagers is a common concern for many parents. Open and honest communication is key to preventing substance abuse. Talk to your child about the risks and consequences of drug and alcohol use, and set clear expectations and boundaries. Encourage them to make healthy choices and seek help if they feel overwhelmed or pressured.

Remember, you can't protect your child from every danger, but by providing guidance, support, and a safe and secure environment, you can help them develop the skills and resilience they need to navigate the world safely.

CHAPTER EIGHT

Gender Issues and Identity

Understanding gender and identity is an important part of growing up and developing into a well-rounded person. As a parent, it's natural to have concerns and questions about how to support your child's gender identity and help them navigate issues related to gender.

First, it's important to recognize that gender is a complex and multifaceted concept that goes beyond traditional notions of male and female. Many people identify as non-binary, genderqueer, or gender non-conforming, and it's important to respect and affirm their identities.

One strategy for supporting your child's gender identity is to use affirming language and pronouns. Ask your child what pronouns they prefer to use and make an effort to use those pronouns consistently. Additionally, avoid making assumptions about your child's gender identity based on their appearance or interests.

It's also important to provide your child with access to resources and support networks. This may include connecting with local LGBTQ+ organizations or seeking out online resources that provide information and support.

It's important to recognize that gender identity can be a sensitive and emotional topic for many people, and it's important to approach these conversations with sensitivity and empathy. Listen to your child's experiences and concerns, and validate their feelings and experiences.

Finally, it's important to recognize that gender identity can be fluid and may change over time.

It's important to support your child in exploring their identity and help them feel comfortable expressing themselves in whatever way feels most authentic to them.

By taking these steps, you can help your child feel supported and affirmed in their gender identity, and help them navigate the complex and often confusing issues related to gender and identity.

Remember, it's never too early or too late to start these conversations and show your child that you love and support them for who they are.

The importance of understanding gender and sexual identity

Understanding gender and sexual identity is crucial in creating a safe and inclusive environment for all individuals.

Unfortunately, there are still many people who lack understanding and awareness around these issues, which can lead to discrimination and mistreatment of those who identify differently than the mainstream.

It's important for parents to talk to their children about gender and sexual identity, as it can help them become more compassionate, accepting, and respectful individuals. Here are a few key points to keep in mind when discussing these topics with your children:

Gender and sexual identity are complex and nuanced: Gender and sexual identity are not binary concepts, and it's important to avoid oversimplifying them. People can identify as male, female, or non-binary, and their sexual orientation can vary widely as well. Encourage your child to ask questions and do their own research, and avoid making assumptions or stereotypes.

Respect people's identities: When someone shares their gender or sexual identity with you, it's important to respect their wishes and use their preferred pronouns and language.

This shows that you value and accept them for who they are, and can help create a safe and supportive environment.

Avoid harmful language and actions: Certain words and actions can be hurtful or disrespectful to people who identify differently than the mainstream.

Teach your child to avoid using slurs or making assumptions about someone's gender or sexual identity, and to speak up if they witness someone else doing so.

Be an ally: Encourage your child to be an ally to those who are marginalized or discriminated against.

This can mean speaking up against discrimination, listening to others' experiences and concerns, and advocating for equal rights and opportunities.

Discussing these issues with your children, you can help create a more accepting and inclusive society, one that values diversity and treats everyone with respect and dignity.

Providing resources for helping your child explore their identity

Understanding one's own identity is an important part of personal growth and development. As parents, it's our responsibility to help our children navigate this process and provide them with the necessary resources and support.

Here are some strategies and resources for helping your child explore their identity:

Encourage self-reflection: Encourage your child to reflect on their feelings and experiences, and help them identify what's important to them. You can also help them identify their strengths and weaknesses, which can help them build confidence and self-esteem.

Expose them to diversity: Expose your child to a variety of cultures, perspectives, and experiences. This can help broaden their understanding of the world and help them appreciate and respect differences.

Provide them with safe spaces: Create a safe and supportive environment where your child feels comfortable exploring their identity. This can be done by providing them with opportunities to express themselves and ensuring that they feel heard and valued.

Seek out supportive communities: Encourage your child to seek out communities that share similar interests or identities. This can help them feel a sense of belonging and support.

Connect them with resources: There are many resources available to help children explore their identity, such as books, online forums, and counseling services. Connect your child with these resources and encourage them to seek out the support they need.

By providing your child with the resources and support they need to explore their identity, you're helping them build a strong sense of self and preparing them for a healthy and fulfilling life.

Addressing common concerns parents have about gender and sexual identity

Gender and sexual identity are complex and multifaceted topics, and it's understandable that as a parent, you may have concerns about how to best support and understand your child's identity.

It's important to remember that every child is unique, and there's no one-size-fits-all approach to understanding and supporting gender and sexual identity.

However, there are some common concerns that parents may have, and it's important to address those concerns with empathy and understanding.

One common concern that parents may have is how to talk to their child about gender and sexual identity. It can be difficult to know where to start, especially if you're not familiar with the terminology or concepts surrounding gender and sexuality.

However, it's important to approach the conversation with an open mind and a willingness to learn. Start by asking your child how they identify and what language they prefer to use. This can help to create a safe and inclusive space for your child to express themselves.

Another common concern that parents may have is how to support their child's gender or sexual identity in a world that may not be accepting or affirming.

This can be especially challenging if your child is facing discrimination or harassment. It's important to be an advocate for your child and to help them find supportive resources and communities.

This may include connecting with LGBTQ+ organizations or seeking out counseling or therapy services.

It's also important to remember that gender and sexual identity can be fluid and may change over time. Your child's identity may evolve as they grow and learn more about themselves, and it's important to support them through that process.

Encourage your child to explore their identity in a safe and supportive environment, and be there to listen and support them along the way.

Ultimately, the most important thing you can do as a parent is to love and support your child unconditionally.

Remember that their identity is valid and deserving of respect, and that you have the power to create a safe and inclusive space for your child to be themselves.

CHAPTER NINE

Questions Likely to Be Asked and How to Answer Them

As a parent or caregiver, it is important to be prepared for any questions that may come up as children begin to explore their sexuality.

Preparing yourself

Here are some of the most frequently asked questions and answers to help you start the conversation:

1. What is sex education and why is it important? Sex education is the process of educating individuals about sexual health, relationships, and behaviors. It is important because it promotes healthy sexual development, reduces the risk of sexually transmitted infections, and empowers individuals to make informed decisions about their sexual lives.
2. At what age should I start talking to my child about sex? It is never too early to start talking to your child about sex. However, the conversation should be age-appropriate and start with basic concepts such as body parts and boundaries. As your child grows, the conversation can become more detailed and nuanced.
3. How do I explain sex to my child? The best way to explain sex to your child is to use age-appropriate language and be honest and direct. Start by explaining the basics, such as

how babies are made, and then build on that knowledge as your child gets older.
4. What do I do if my child asks me a question I don't know the answer to? If you don't know the answer to a question, it's okay to admit it. You can tell your child that you don't know the answer but that you will find out together. This can be a great opportunity to learn and explore together.
5. How do I talk to my child about consent? Consent is a crucial part of any sexual relationship. Start by teaching your child about boundaries and that it is important to always ask for permission before engaging in any sexual activity.
6. What do I do if my child is being bullied because of their sexual orientation or gender identity? Bullying can have serious consequences for a child's mental and emotional well-being. If your child is being bullied, it is important to provide a safe and supportive environment at home and seek help from school officials or a counselor.
7. How do I talk to my child about pornography? Pornography is a sensitive and complex issue. It is important to explain that pornography is not a realistic portrayal of sexual relationships and that it can have negative consequences on a person's self-esteem and sexual development.
8. How do I address masturbation with my child? Masturbation is a normal and healthy part of sexual development. You can explain that it is a private behavior and provide guidance on how to do it safely.
9. How do I talk to my child about birth control? Birth control is an important part of sexual health and can prevent

unintended pregnancy. Explain the different types of birth control and encourage your child to make informed decisions.
10. How do I address sexual health issues such as sexually transmitted infections (STIs)? It is important to teach your child about sexual health and the risks associated with unprotected sex. You can explain the importance of practicing safe sex and getting regular STI testing.

Questions and Answers

- What is sex? Answer: Sex is an act between two consenting adults that involves physical intimacy, such as touching, kissing, and genital contact.
- What is puberty? Answer: Puberty is the time in life when a person's body starts to change and develop to become an adult. It usually begins around age 8-13 for girls and 9-14 for boys.
- How does a baby get inside a woman's belly? Answer: When a man and a woman have sex, the man's sperm can fertilize the woman's egg, which can then grow into a baby inside her belly.
- What is consent? Answer: Consent means that both people involved in a sexual activity agree to it and understand what they are doing. It is important to always ask for consent and respect someone's decision if they say no.
- How do I know if someone likes me? Answer: It can be hard to tell if someone likes you, but some signs might include them wanting to spend time with you, talking to you a lot, or complimenting you.

- Can I get pregnant from kissing or oral sex? Answer: No, you cannot get pregnant from kissing or oral sex. Pregnancy can only happen when sperm from a man's penis enters a woman's vagina and fertilizes an egg.
- What is safe sex? Answer: Safe sex is when you use protection, such as condoms or birth control, to reduce the risk of getting a sexually transmitted infection (STI) or unintended pregnancy.
- How can I talk to my partner about using protection? Answer: It's important to talk to your partner about using protection before having sex. You can say something like, "I want to make sure we're both safe, can we use a condom?" or "Let's make sure we have birth control so we don't have to worry about getting pregnant."
- What is an STI? Answer: An STI is an infection that is spread through sexual contact. Some common STIs include chlamydia, gonorrhea, and herpes.
- Can you tell if someone has an STI just by looking at them? Answer: No, you cannot tell if someone has an STI just by looking at them. Many people with STIs have no symptoms, so it's important to get tested regularly if you are sexually active.
- How do I know if I have an STI? Answer: The only way to know for sure if you have an STI is to get tested. Many STIs have no symptoms, so it's important to get tested regularly if you are sexually active.
- Can you catch an STI from oral sex? Answer: Yes, you can catch an STI from oral sex. It's important to use protection, such as a dental dam or condom, to reduce the risk of getting an STI.

- What is masturbation? Answer: Masturbation is when a person touches or stimulates their own body in a sexual way to feel pleasure.
- Is masturbation normal? Answer: Yes, masturbation is a normal and healthy part of sexuality for many people.
- What is pornography? Answer: Pornography is images, videos, or stories that are created to sexually arouse people. And you should know they can be harmful to you because they are actually harmful for me too.
- Is it okay to watch pornography? Answer: No baby (or whatever sweet name you call your child) It's important to remember that pornography is not real life and can sometimes give people unrealistic expectations about sex. It's also important to make sure that you are not watching anything that is illegal or harmful to others.

Providing guidance on how to handle difficult or uncomfortable questions

So you've started talking to your tweens about sex and relationships, and they're asking some tough questions. It can be uncomfortable, but it's important to keep the conversation going. Here are some tips for handling those awkward or challenging questions:

Be honest: If you don't know the answer, say so. Don't try to make something up or avoid the question. You can always do some research together or consult a trusted resource.

Stay calm: Try not to react with shock or disapproval to their questions. Keep your tone neutral and non-judgmental, so they feel safe to ask anything.

Validate their feelings: Let them know that their questions are important and normal. You might say, "I'm so glad you asked that. It shows that you're curious and interested in learning."

Use age-appropriate language: Make sure your responses are tailored to their level of understanding. You don't need to use technical or graphic language unless they specifically ask for it.

Keep it brief: Don't overwhelm them with too much information at once. Give simple, concise answers and allow them to ask follow-up questions if they want more details.

Encourage open communication: Let them know that they can always come to you with questions, even if it feels embarrassing or uncomfortable. Remind them that you're there to support and guide them.

Know your resources: Have a list of trusted books, websites, or professionals that you can recommend if they want to learn more.

Here's an example of how you can apply these tips in a real-life situation:

Your tween asks, "What's oral sex?"

You might respond: "Oral sex is when one person uses their mouth to stimulate their partner's genitals. It's a form of sexual activity that some people enjoy. It's important to remember that any sexual activity should be consensual, meaning both partners agree to it. Does that answer your question?"

Remember, talking to your tweens about sex and relationships can be a little awkward, but it's crucial to their healthy development. By using these tips, you can create a safe and supportive environment for them to learn and grow.

CONCLUSION

Final Thoughts

Congratulations! You've made it to the end of the book. By now, you should have a better understanding of sex and relationships, and how to talk to your tween about them.

Here are some key takeaways from the book:

Communication is key. It's important to have ongoing conversations with your child about sex and relationships so that they feel comfortable coming to you with questions and concerns.

Be honest and age-appropriate. When answering your child's questions, be honest and provide information that is appropriate for their age and level of understanding.

Talk about consent. Teach your child about the importance of consent in all types of relationships, and that it's okay to say no or change their mind.

Address common misconceptions. Help your child understand that everyone's experience with sex and relationships is different, and that there is no "normal" or "right" way to feel.

Provide resources. There are many books, websites, and organizations that offer additional information and support for both parents and tweens.

Remember, sex education is an ongoing conversation that should continue throughout your child's life. Don't be afraid to ask questions and seek out resources to help you navigate these sometimes tricky topics.

Below are some additional resources that you may find helpful:

Planned Parenthood: A trusted resource for sexual health information and services.

Advocates for Youth: A nonprofit organization dedicated to promoting adolescent sexual health and rights.

Thank you for taking the time to read this book and for your commitment to providing your child with the knowledge and support they need to make informed decisions about their sexual health and relationships.

Printed in Great Britain
by Amazon